I Can Make

TOYS

Emily Reid

WINDMILL
BOOKS
New York

Published in 2016 by **Windmill Books**, an Imprint of Rosen Publishing
29 East 21st Street, New York, NY 10010

Developed and produced for Rosen by BlueAppleWorks Inc.

Creative Director: Melissa McClellan
Managing Editor for BlueAppleWorks: Melissa McClellan
Designer: T.J. Choleva
Photo Research: Jane Reid
Editor: Janice Dyer
Craft Artisans: Jerrie McClellan (p. 8, 12, 18, 22, 28, 30);
    Jane Yates (p. 10, 16, 20, 26); Sarah Hodgson (p. 14, 24)

Photo Credits: cover center image Africa Studio/Shutterstock; cover background image, title page
background Ocskay Bence/Shutterstock; cover insets, title page, TOC, p. 6 bottom, 8–9, 10–11, 12–13,
14–15, 16–17, 18–19, 20–21, 22–23, 24–25, 26–27, 28-29, 30 Austen Photography; p. 4 left, 5 first row Photka/
Dreamstime; p. 4 right Ermolaevamariya/Dreamstime; p. 4 right bottom Richard Thomas/Dreamstime;
p. 5 first row right Ghassan Safi/Dreamstime; p. 5 second row left Design56/Dreamstime; p. 5 second row
middle Christian Bertrand/Dreamstime; p. 5 second row right Fuse/Thinkstock; p. 5 third row left Vasily
Kovalev/Dreamstime; p. 5 third row middle Sergey Mostovoy/Dreamstime; p. 5 third row right (left to right)
Crackerclips/Dreamstime; Les Cunliffe/Dreamstime; Jerryb8/Dreamstime; p. 5 fourth row left Romval/
Dreamstime; p. 5 fourth row right (left to right clockwise) Arinahabich08/Dreamstime; antpkr/Thinkstock;
Kelpfish/Dreamstime; Jirk4/Dreamstime; Gradts/Dreamstime; sodapix sodapix/Thinkstock; p. 6 top Jakub
Krechowicz/Dreamstime; p. 6 middle Steveheap/Dreamstime; p. 7 top Konstantin Kirillov/Dreamstime; p. 9
top right Africa Studio/Shutterstock; p. 11 bottom left Jose Manuel Gelpi Diaz/Dreamstime; p. 11 top right
4x6/iStockphoto; p. 13 top right Dr Ajay Kumar Singh/Shutterstock; p. 15 top right Serrnovik/Dreamstime;
p. 17 top right Rossco/Dreamstime; p. 19 top right Milosluz/Dreamstime; p. 21 top right Monkey Business
Images/Shutterstock; p. 23 top right Thomas Vieth/Dreamstime; p. 25 top right Alekosa/Dreamstime; p. 27
top right Srki66/Dreamstime; p. 29 top right Claudia Paulussen/Shutterstock

Cataloging-in-Publication-Data
Reid, Emily.
I can make toys / by Emily Reid.
p. cm. — (Makerspace projects)
Includes index.
ISBN 978-1-4777-5645-4 (pbk.)
ISBN 978-1-4777-5644-7 (6 pack)
ISBN 978-1-4777-5568-6 (library binding)
1. Toy making — Juvenile literature.
2. Handicraft — Juvenile literature.
3. Toys — Juvenile literature. I. Title.
TT174.R45 2016
745.59'2—d23

Manufactured in the United States of America
CPSIA Compliance Information: Batch #WS15WM: For Further Information contact: Rosen Publishing, New York, New York at 1-800-237-9932

CONTENTS

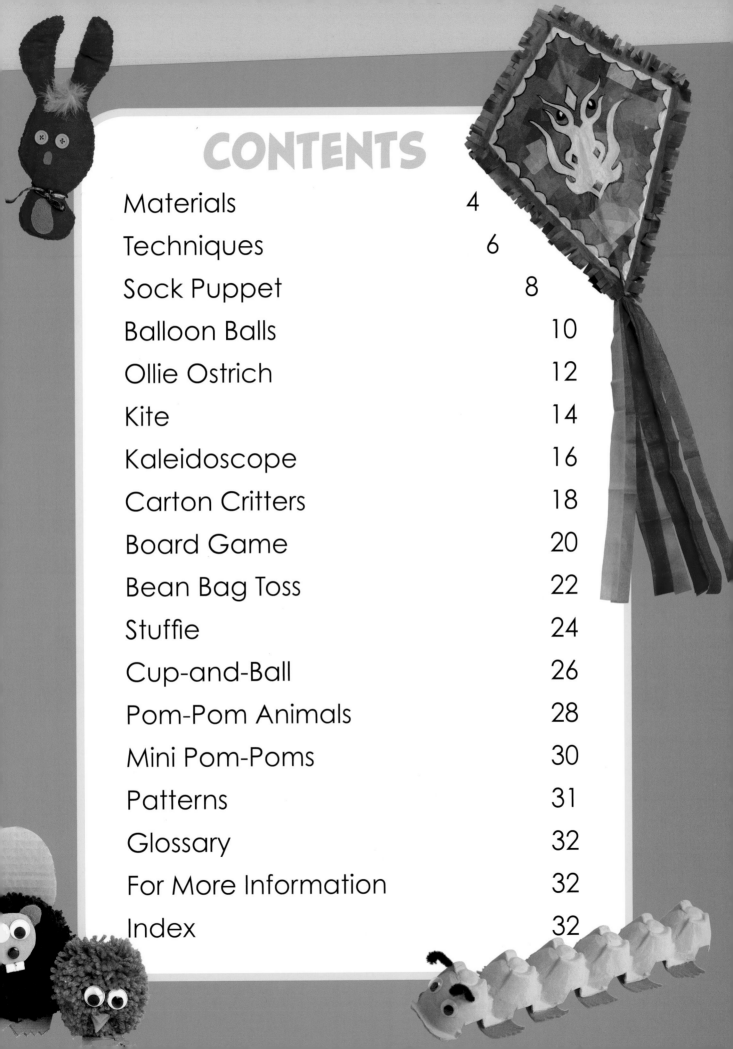

MATERIALS

A makerspace is a space to think and be creative. You can dedicate a space for your makerspace, or make one as you need it. You may already have many of the basic supplies for your makerspace. You can purchase whatever else you need at a craft store or dollar store. If you don't have a dedicated area, make a portable makerspace by organizing your supplies in boxes or plastic bins and pull them out when you want to create.

A note about patterns

Many of the toys in this book use patterns or **templates**. Trace the pattern, cut the pattern, and then place it on the material you want to cut out. You can either tape it in place and cut both the pattern and material, or trace around the pattern onto the material and then cut it out.

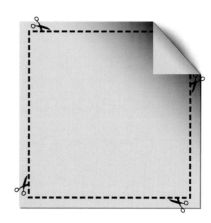

RECYCLABLES

You can make many of the toys in this book with materials found around the house. Save recyclables (newspapers, cardboard boxes, mailing tubes, cereal boxes, tin cans, and more) to use in your craft projects.
Use your imagination and have fun!

A note about measurements

Measurements are given in U.S. form with metric in brackets. The metric conversion is rounded to make it easier to measure.

PAINT AND MARKERS

CRAFT THREAD

DECORATIVE TAPE

BUTTONS

FEATHERS

FELT

GLUE AND TAPE

PAPER

TOOLS

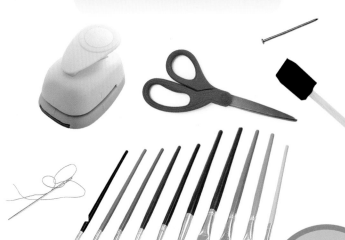

TECHNIQUES

Have fun while making your toys! Be creative. Your project does not have to look just like the one in this book. If you don't have a certain material, think of something similar you could use.

The following techniques will help you create your crafts.

Using your creativity to make crafts is a very rewarding activity. When you are finished, you can say with great pride, **"I made that!"**

THREADING A NEEDLE

Threading a needle can be frustrating. The following tips will help.

- Cut more thread than you think you will need.
- Wet one end of the thread in your mouth.
- Poke it through the needle opening.
- Pull some of the thread through until you have an even amount and make a double knot.
- If you are using thicker thread like embroidery thread, do not double up the thread. Just pull a small amount through and make the knot at the other end.

EASIEST METHOD

- Use a metal needle threader.
- Push the metal threader through the needle hole, put the thread through the loop and then pull the needle threader back through the needle.

Once the thread is in the loop, pull the loop back through the needle.

Put the thread through the loop.

SEWING FABRIC

The whipstitch works great with felt. It is used to sew two pieces together.

- Place the needle and knotted thread in between the two pieces of felt and up through the top layer of felt.
- Take the needle behind both layers of felt at point 1.
- Pull the needle through both layers of felt at point 2.
- Continue stitching until finished.

SEWING BUTTONS

- Thread the needle.
- Double over the thread until you have equal amounts on either side and tie a knot.
- Run the needle through the fabric where the button will go.
- Push the needle from the back to the front through the first button hole.
- Take the needle through each hole of the button a couple of times.
- Tie a small knot under the button and trim the extra thread.

USING COLLAGE

You can decorate your toy using the collage technique. Arrange and glue cut-up pieces of tissue paper, magazine pages, or wrapping paper in an interesting pattern.

- Standard craft glue works best if it is **diluted** with a little water.
- Use a paintbrush to spread some of the glue onto a small part of your project. Press the paper into the glue.
- When you are finished gluing the paper, cover it with a thin layer of glue to seal the paper.
- Make sure to use glue that dries clear.

You can also use specialty glues which can be found in most crafting stores.

FOLDING CARDBOARD

Cardboard is easier to fold if you **score** the fold lines first:

- Place a ruler along the line you want to fold.
- Set a blunt tip* on the surface of the cardboard against the ruler.
- Press and pull the blunt tip along the ruler.
- Do not cut through the cardboard.
- Bend the cardboard at the indentation created.

*scoring tool (you can use anything that has a blunt tip: a **retracted** ballpoint pen, dull pencil, screwdriver)

BE PREPARED

- Read through the instructions and make sure you have all the materials you need.
- Cover your work area with newspaper or cardboard.
- Clean up your makerspace when you are finished making your project.

BE SAFE

- Ask for help when you need it.
- Ask for permission to borrow tools.
- Be careful when using knives, scissors, and sewing needles.

SOCK PUPPET

Put on a play with your own sock puppet creations. Use your imagination to create a whole cast of characters.

You'll Need

- ✔ Cardboard
- ✔ Yarn
- ✔ Scissors
- ✔ Sock
- ✔ Tapestry needle
- ✔ Glue
- ✔ Googly eyes (2)
- ✔ Felt (white)
- ✔ Buttons (2)
- ✔ Needle
- ✔ Thread

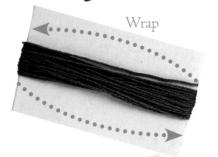

Wrap

Tie

Cut

Pull yarn through.

Tie double knot.

1 Make the hair first. Cut a piece of cardboard 6 inches (15 cm) wide. Wind yarn around the cardboard about 50 times. Cut the end. Cut a 12-inch (30 cm) piece of yarn and tie it around the center of the yarn loop.

2 Turn the cardboard over. Cut the yarn loop in the center of the board opposite the knot on the front of the board.

3 Attach the hair to the sock. Put one end of the yarn on a tapestry needle and pull it through the sock near the toe end. Repeat with the other yarn end. Tie the two yarn ends together and make a double knot.

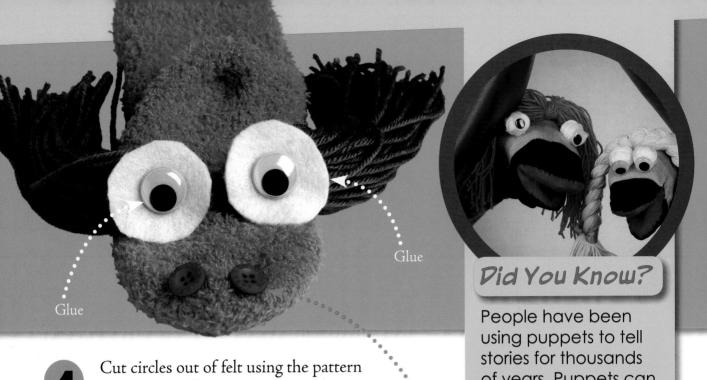

Glue

Glue

Glue

Cut circles out of felt using the pattern on page 31. Glue googly eyes to the circles. Glue the circles to the sock.

4

Did You Know?

People have been using puppets to tell stories for thousands of years. Puppets can communicate ideas and entertain.

Sew buttons.

5 Thread a needle. Tie a knot at the bottom. Sew two buttons at the tip of the sock.

Sew

6 Cut out a felt tongue using the pattern on page 31. Sew the tongue to the sock on the underside of the sock.

Tip

To thread a tapestry needle, wrap a small amount of tape around the end of the wool, and pull it through. Cut off the tape.

BALLOON BALLS

Use your balloon ball to play a game! Stand in a circle with two or more players. The goal is to keep the ball off the ground for as long as possible using your feet. You can use any part of your body except for your hands to keep the ball up.

You'll Need

✔ Paper
✔ Scissors
✔ Tape
✔ Balloons (2)
✔ Sand, gravel, or rice

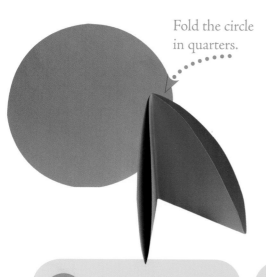

Fold the circle in quarters.

Cut out one section of the circle.

Pour the gravel into the balloon.

1 Make a paper funnel. Cut a circle out of a letter size piece of paper. Fold it in half, and then in quarters.

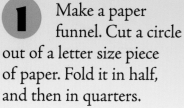

2 Cut a triangle out of the circle. Fold and tape your funnel.

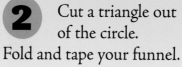

3 Place the funnel into the opening of the ballon. Ask someone to hold it for you or tape them together. Pour the sand gravel or rice into the balloon. Jiggle the balloon to make room for more sand.

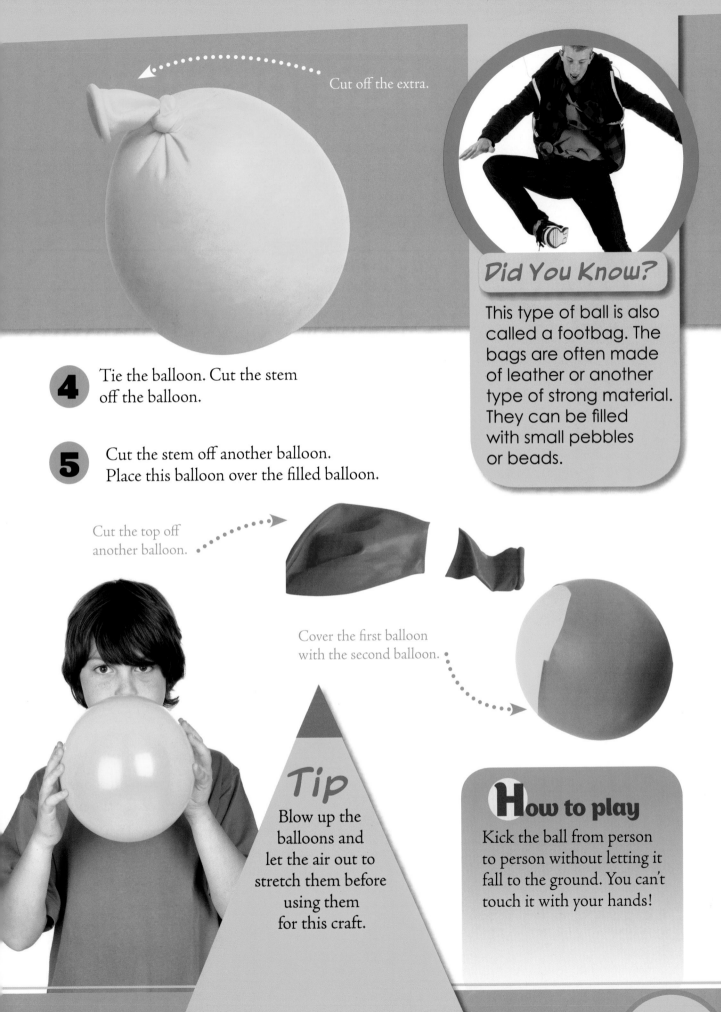

Cut off the extra.

4 Tie the balloon. Cut the stem off the balloon.

5 Cut the stem off another balloon. Place this balloon over the filled balloon.

Did You Know?

This type of ball is also called a footbag. The bags are often made of leather or another type of strong material. They can be filled with small pebbles or beads.

Cut the top off another balloon.

Cover the first balloon with the second balloon.

Tip

Blow up the balloons and let the air out to stretch them before using them for this craft.

How to play

Kick the ball from person to person without letting it fall to the ground. You can't touch it with your hands!

OLLIE OSTRICH

A marionette is a puppet controlled using wires or strings. Marionettes are operated by a puppeteer who is often hidden during the performance.

You'll Need

- ✔ Styrofoam balls (1 large and 1 small)
- ✔ Glue
- ✔ Colored paper
- ✔ Beading wire
- ✔ Circle punch (1 inch)
- ✔ Feathers
- ✔ Fuzzy boa
- ✔ Googly eyes (2)
- ✔ Plastic containers (2)
- ✔ Duct tape
- ✔ String
- ✔ Sticks (2)
- ✔ Scissors
- ✔ Nail
- ✔ Nut (optional)

Glue

Tape

Glue

Glue

Glue

1 Decorate the small styrofoam ball by gluing feathers all over it. Glue on two googly eyes. Cut out a yellow beak using the pattern on page 31. Fold the beak in half. Make a slight indent in the styrofoam for the beak. Glue the beak.

2 Punch colored paper circles using the circle punch. Glue them onto the large styrofoam ball. Cut the tips off large feathers for wings. Tape them to the styrofoam ball. Cover the end of the wings with circles.

3 Cut the boa into two pieces, one shorter piece for the neck and one piece twice as long for the legs.

Make a hole.

Bend each piece of wire in half.

Use empty yogurt, butter or margarine containers for the feet. Wash and dry them first.

Did You Know?

Marionettes have been used for entertainment since ancient times. String is used to control the puppet's arms, legs, and other body parts.

4 Make six wire staples to fasten the boa pieces to the styrofoam balls. Cut beading wire into ½-inch (1.3 cm) pieces and bend in half.

5 Make two feet out of plastic containers. Use a nail to make a small hole in the bottom of each container. Wrap decorative tape around the container.

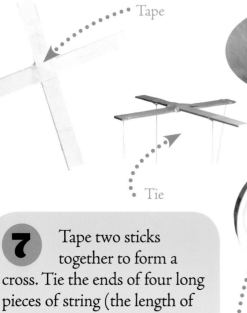

Tape

Staple

Tie

Nut

Pull boa through and tie.

6 Attach the neck boa to the head using a staple. Attach the other end of the neck to the body. Attach the legs by folding the remaining piece of boa in half and staple the middle to the body. Put the end of the legs through the hole in each container. Tie a knot. (Optional: before tying the knot, add a heavy nut to the boa.)

7 Tape two sticks together to form a cross. Tie the ends of four long pieces of string (the length of your arms) to the back of each boa leg, the top of the head and back of the body. Tie the other end of each string to each end of the cross. Adjust strings so they hold the ostrich upright. Tape in place.

KITE

Kites are made of a light frame that is covered with paper, cloth, or plastic. The kite's tail helps keep it stable in the air. Use your imagination to decorate your kite and then take it flying!

You'll Need

- ✔ Paper (large rectangular sheets of craft paper)
- ✔ Pencil
- ✔ Scissors
- ✔ Masking tape
- ✔ Newspaper
- ✔ Glue
- ✔ Tissue paper
- ✔ String

Fold

Fold

Fold

Fold

Roll the paper tightly.

Tape

Fold

1 Fold (gently) your craft paper lengthwise to find the center point. Draw a line down the center. Fold the top to make two triangles.

2 Fold the sides from the bottom center point to the outside point. Repeat for the other side. You have now made the basic kite shape.

3 Make paper **dowels** with newspaper. Roll the newspaper from corner to corner as tight as you can. Tape it to secure the paper dowels.

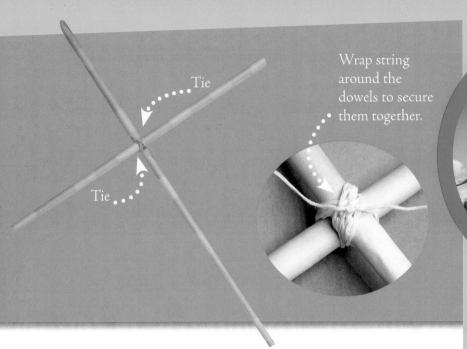

Tie

Tie

Wrap string around the dowels to secure them together.

Did You Know?

Kites were invented in China. They were made from silk fabric and the frame was made from bamboo. Today's kites are often made to look like flying birds, insects, or mythical creatures.

4 Cut one dowel to match the length of the kite top to bottom. Cut another dowel to match the width from side to side. Attach the dowels together with string. Wrap the string around many times to reinforce it.

5 Tape the dowel frame to the inside of the paper kite.

Use lots of tape to secure the frame to the paper.

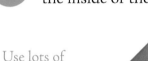

8 Tape the tail to the back of the kite. Attach a roll of string to the back of the cross and you are ready to fly your kite!

Tie your string here.

Tape the tail to the kite.

Go fly a kite

Flying a kite is great fun on a windy day. It is best to fly it in a park with lots of open space. Run with the kite while letting the string out. Once the wind has it, let more string out and watch it soar!

Make a tail.

6 Decorate the kite with paint, collage or both! Use the technique shown on page 7.

7 Add a tail by cutting strips of tissue paper. Tape them together.

KALEIDOSCOPE

Kaleidoscopes are made with mirrors and colored objects. As you look in one end of the cylinder, light from the other end reflects off the mirrors. Make your own kaleidoscope to create beautiful patterns!

You'll Need

- ✔ Cardboard tube (paper towel tube or chip container with bottom removed by an adult)
- ✔ Tape
- ✔ Colored paper
- ✔ Card stock
- ✔ Reflective silver card stock
- ✔ Clear plastic container
- ✔ Scissors
- ✔ Colored transparent beads, small sequins

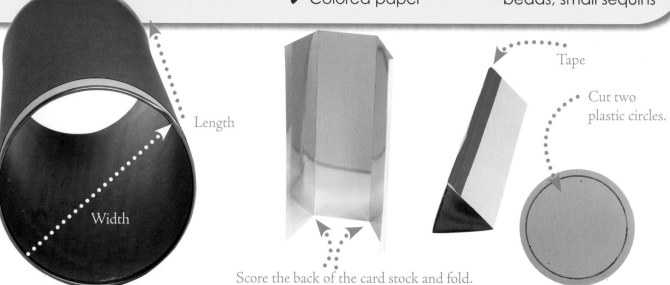

Length

Width

Score the back of the card stock and fold.

Tape

Cut two plastic circles.

1 Cover the cardboard tube with colored paper. Measure the cardboard tube. Subtract ¼ inch (.06 cm) from the width of the tube. Use this measurement to mark the back of the silver card stock. Make three marks at this interval.

2 Score the card stock at the three marks. Fold it at the scored marks. Trim the card stock leaving an extra lip for taping. Tape the card stock closed into a triangle. The shiny side should be on the inside.

3 Trace around the end of the tube on card stock. Cut it out leaving extra room. Use this as a template to cut two circles out of clear plastic. Cut notches all around the three circles.

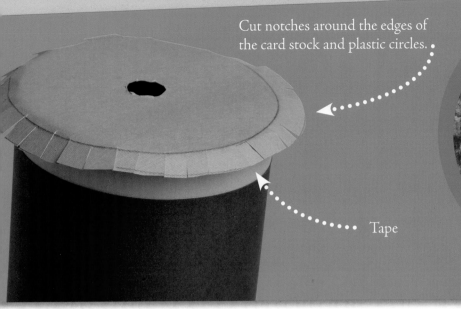

Cut notches around the edges of the card stock and plastic circles.

Tape

Did You Know?

The kaleidoscope was invented in 1815. It was first used as a scientific tool, then it was made into a toy. The word "kaleidoscope" means "observer of beautiful forms" in Greek.

4 Punch a hole in the center of the card stock circle. Tape it to one end of the tube. Slide the triangle into the cardboard tube.

The plastic rests on top of the tube, taped in place.

5 Fit one of the plastic circles inside the tube, resting on the triangle.

Wrap a cardboard sleeve around the tube and tape the ends.

6 Fill the tube with colored transparent beads and sequins almost to the top.

Fill with beads and sequins.

Tape

How to play

Hold the cardboard sleeve and turn the tube. Look through the hole and watch beautiful colored patterns emerge!

7 Cover with the other plastic circle (or the lid if using a chip container) and tape in place. Wrap a piece of cardboard around the tube and tape the ends together. Do not tape it to the tube.

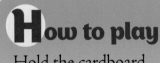

CARTON CRITTERS

You can make all kinds of different insects out of egg cartons. Read on to learn how!

You'll Need

- ✔ Cardboard egg carton
- ✔ Scissors
- ✔ Craft paint
- ✔ Brush
- ✔ Paper for tracing
- ✔ Felt
- ✔ Scissors

- ✔ Pushpin
- ✔ Glue
- ✔ Chenille stems
- ✔ Googly eyes
- ✔ Black pom-poms
- ✔ Black marker
- ✔ Tape

CENTIPEDE

Cut the top off.

Cut down the middle.

Cut out ten feet.

Glue

Trim around the edges.

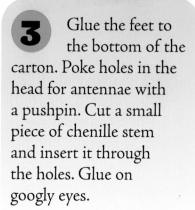

1 Cut the top off the egg carton. Cut the egg carton up the center lengthwise. Trim on both sides as close to the edges as you can.

2 Paint the carton with craft paint. Use one color or make a pattern. Cut 10 feet out of felt using the pattern on page 31.

3 Glue the feet to the bottom of the carton. Poke holes in the head for antennae with a pushpin. Cut a small piece of chenille stem and insert it through the holes. Glue on googly eyes.

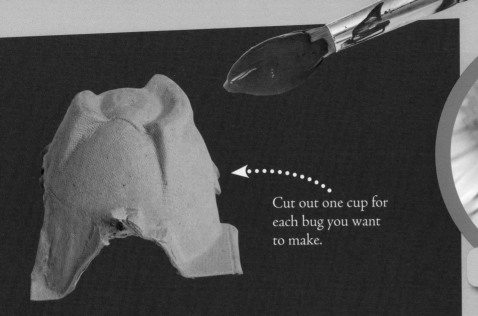

Cut out one cup for each bug you want to make.

Did You Know?

There are over 1 million different species of insects around the world. You can often identify the species by looking at the color patterns.

LADYBUG OR SPIDER

1 Cut individual egg cups from the carton. For the ladybug, paint the cup red. For the spider, paint the cup black.

Bend the legs.

2 For the ladybug, add black dots and wing lines with a black marker when the red paint dries.

Glue a felt mouth.

Tape

3 Glue two googly eyes to a black pom-pom. Glue the pom-pom to the egg cup. Cut out a white felt mouth for the spider and glue it below the eyes.

Tip
The end cups on the egg carton work best for individual critters.

4 Make legs by cutting chenille stems. The ladybug needs six legs. The spider needs eight longer legs. Make holes in the carton with a pushpin. Push the chenille stems through the hole. Bend the tip and tape to the carton.

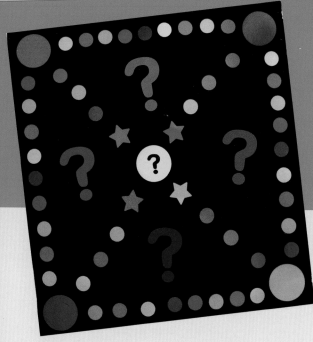

BOARD GAME

In board games, you move tokens around a board according to rules. You can create your own board game. Invent a game and then have fun playing with your friends.

You'll Need

✔ Cardboard
✔ Colored paper
✔ Scissors
✔ Glue
✔ Stickers
✔ Fastener

Attach the fastener loosely so the spinner can spin.

Decorate circles with stickers.

You could put numbers on the circles.

1 Decide what your game will be. Design a board for the game to be played on. Make shapes for players to move their tokens around the board. You can cut out squares or circles from colored paper and glue them to a piece of cardboard.

2 Create tokens to move around the board. To make cardboard tokens, cut out circles from colored cardboard and decorate them with stickers.

3 Decide how many moves a player can take. To make a spinner wheel, cut a square of cardboard. Place circles to match the board. Cut out an arrow and attach it to the spinner with a fastener.

Write tasks.

4 Make some cards for when you land on specially marked places on the board. Cut colored paper into equally-sized rectangles. Add stickers to the front. On the back, write things that will happen when a player picks up a card, such as getting an extra turn or a question to answer.

Did You Know?

People have been playing board games since ancient times. There are many different kinds of board games. Some have simple rules, while others are very complex. One of the best things about board games is that you get to spend time with your friends or family while playing.

5 Write down the rules and object of the game so that everyone knows how to play.

Play your game!

Explain the rules to your friends and play a game. After you play, think about ways to make the game even better.

BEAN BAG TOSS

In this fun game, players take turns throwing bags of beans at a raised platform with holes. Make your own game, then play with your friends!

You'll Need

- ✔ Felt
- ✔ Scissors
- ✔ Needle
- ✔ Thread
- ✔ Dried beans or peas
- ✔ Duct tape
- ✔ Stickers
- ✔ Number stickers or marker

- ✔ 2 pieces of cardboard or foam core measuring 18 x 24 inches (46 x 61 cm)
- ✔ Cardboard or foam core measuring 9 x 12 inches (23 x 30 cm)

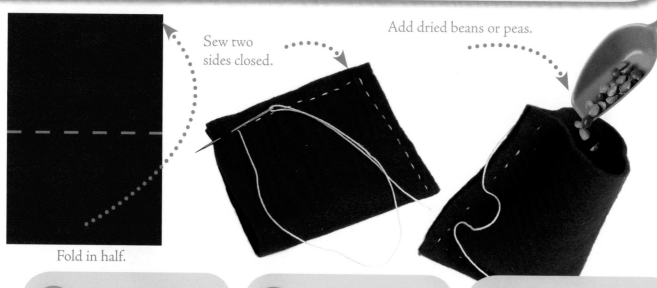

Fold in half.

Sew two sides closed.

Add dried beans or peas.

Make a knot.

1 Cut two or more pieces of felt into a rectangle shape. Use the pattern on page 31. Fold each felt piece in half.

2 Thread a needle with craft thread. Sew the edges together using the whipstitch technique shown on page 6. Leave one end open.

3 Pour beans or peas into the open side. Do not fill it too full. Sew across the open end. Finish by making a knot and then trim off the leftover thread.

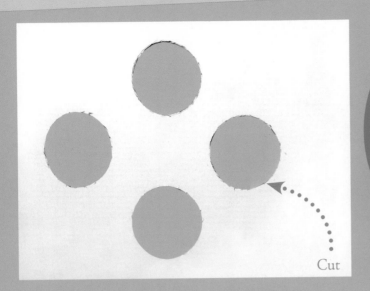

Cut

4 Mark and cut large holes on one large piece of the foam core or cardboard. Make sure the bags will fit through the holes.

Tape

5 Decorate the front of the target board with stickers. Use stickers of numbers or draw them with a marker.

Make a border with tape.

Let's Play

Players take turns throwing the bean bags at the board with holes. The player who reaches the score of 21 first wins.

Tape

Tape

6 Tape the piece of cardboard with holes to another piece of cardboard the same size. Tape both of these pieces to a third bottom piece that is half the size of the other two.

STUFFIE

Stuffed toys are made from fabric that is stuffed with soft materials. They are often made to look like animals or cartoon figures. You can make your own stuffed toy!

You'll Need

- ✔ Felt
- ✔ Paper
- ✔ Pencil or marker
- ✔ Scissors
- ✔ Pins
- ✔ Needle
- ✔ Thread
- ✔ Stuffing or tissue paper
- ✔ Chenille stem
- ✔ Fake fur or fuzzy boa
- ✔ Buttons
- ✔ Ribbon

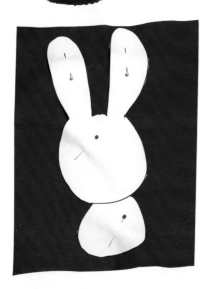

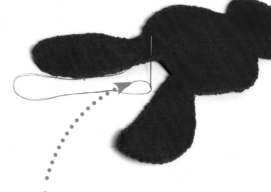

Leave an opening.

1 Make your own pattern. Draw an animal or monster on paper. Cut out the drawing. Pin the pattern to your material.

2 Cut around the pattern to cut out the pieces of felt. Pin the pattern to a second piece of felt either the same color as the first or a different color. Cut it out.

3 Sew the two pieces together. Leave a small opening.

Push the stuffing with a pencil.

YELLOW PENCIL HB

4 Insert stuffing or crumpled tissue paper through the small opening. Use a pencil to get the stuffing into hard-to-reach places.

5 For bendable ears, arms or legs, insert a chenille stem. Pinch the opening together and sew it closed.

6 Sew a scrap of fake fur or boa to the head. Sew buttons for eyes. Glue bits of felt for a nose and stomach. Wrap a ribbon around the stuffie to make a scarf.

Tip Save bits of fabric from other craft projects to reuse them rather than throwing them out.

CUP-AND-BALL

This ancient game is traditionally made out of wood. There are various versions of it throughout the world. Some versions involve a ring and pin.

You'll Need

- ✔ Paper
- ✔ Scissors
- ✔ Tape
- ✔ Decorative tape (optional)
- ✔ Cup (paper or styrofoam)
- ✔ Nail
- ✔ String
- ✔ Button
- ✔ Screw eye hook
- ✔ Pushpin
- ✔ Glue
- ✔ Small ball (styrofoam or Ping-Pong ball)

Cut a fringe along the top of the paper.

Trim the fringe to fit the bottom of the cup.

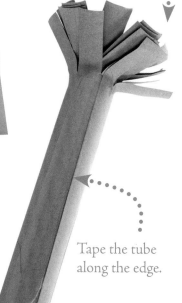

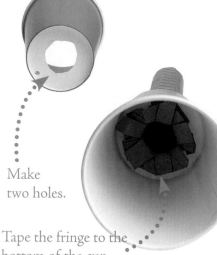

Make two holes.

Tape the fringe to the bottom of the cup.

Tape the tube along the edge.

1 First make the handle. Cut out a 7-inch x 12-inch (18 cm x 31 cm) piece of heavy paper. Make a fringe along the top edge by making 1-inch (2.5 cm) cuts about every ¼ inch (0.6 cm).

2 Roll the paper into a tube shape. Tape. Optional: cover the tube with decorative tape.

3 Use a nail to make a hole in the bottom of the cup. Make the center hole bigger with scissors. Pull the handle through the large hole and tape the fringe to the bottom of the cup.

Pull string through the hole in the cup. Tie a button to the end of the string.

Pull the string until the button is snug against the bottom of the cup.

Did You Know?

Kendama is a very similar game that uses three cups and a spike. It is very popular in Japan.

4 Cut a piece of string at least three times as long as your cup. Pull one end of the string through the hole in the cup. Tie the string to a button and pull the string back out of the cup until the button is snug against the bottom of the cup. Tape over it.

Screw the eye hook into the ball.

5 Tie the other end of the string onto an eye hook.

6 Poke a small hole in a the ball with a pushpin. Add a dab of glue, then screw in the eye hook.

Let's play!

The goal of the game is to get the ball into the cup. Hold the cup by the handle and let the ball hang freely. Toss the ball up by jerking the arm holding the toy. Try to catch the ball in the cup. How many times can you do it in a row?

POM-POM ANIMALS

You can make all kinds of creatures and animals from pom-poms. You can buy pom-poms or make your own.

You'll Need

- ✔ Cardboard
- ✔ Paper for tracing
- ✔ Scissors
- ✔ Yarn
- ✔ Googly eyes
- ✔ Glue
- ✔ Felt
- ✔ Button

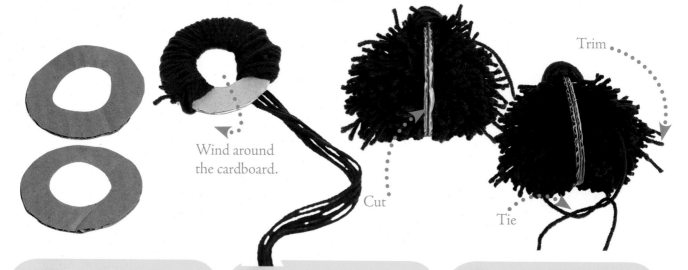

Wind around the cardboard.

Cut

Tie

Trim

1 Using the pattern on page 31, cut out two cardboard donut shapes. Place them together.

2 Take four long strands of yarn and start winding them around the donut. Wind a thick layer. The more yarn the thicker the pom-pom. If you run out of yarn, just start winding new strands.

3 Place scissors between the two cardboard donuts and cut the yarn. Cut a piece of yarn and wind it between the two cardboard donuts. Pull the yarn tight and make a double knot. Remove the cardboard. Trim the pom-pom so it is even.

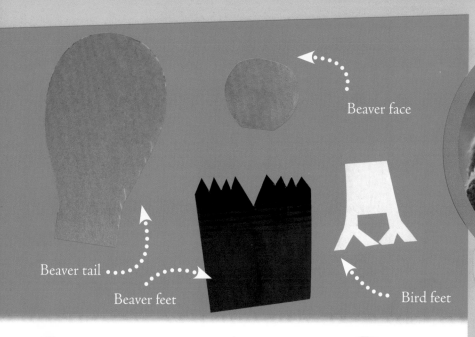

Beaver face

Beaver tail

Beaver feet

Bird feet

Did You Know?

The word pom-pom comes from the French word "pompon." Pom-poms are used as decorations on hats and other clothing.

4 Cut out the cardboard pieces for the beaver and bird using the patterns on page 31. Glue the cardboard feet pieces to the pom-poms.

Tail

5 Cut out the felt pieces for the beaver using the patterns on page 31. Glue the felt pieces to the back of the cardboard face. Glue the googly eyes to the face. Glue the button nose to the face. Attach the face to the pom-pom with glue.

Glue one wing on each side.

Glue the googly eyes.

6 Cut out the felt pieces for the bird using the patterns on page 31. Glue the felt pieces to the pom-pom. Glue the googly eyes to the pom-pom.

Fold the beak in half and glue.

Tip

You can reuse the cardboard pom-pom templates if you tape them back together.

MINI POM-POMS

You can make pom-pom creatures with pom-poms bought from a store as well. These pom-poms make adorable mini animals and bugs!

You'll Need

- ✔ Pom-poms (assorted sizes and colors)
- ✔ Construction paper
- ✔ Felt
- ✔ Googly eyes
- ✔ Glue
- ✔ Chenille stems
- ✔ Black marker

Felt

Make antennae from yarn.

Cut wings from construction paper.

Felt

Felt

Make legs from chenille stems.

1 Bear: glue six pom-poms together. Glue googly eyes to the head. Draw a mouth with black marker. Cut ears out of felt and glue them to the head. Caterpillar: glue five small pom-poms together. Glue googly eyes to the head. Cut and glue two small pieces of yarn for antennae.

2 Bee: glue four small and one large pom-pom together. Trace the pattern piece on page 31. Place the pattern over black construction paper and cut out four wings. Glue the wings in place as shown. Cut six small legs from pipe cleaners and glue them to bottom piece and then to the bottom of the body.

3 Dog: glue a white pom-pom between two black pom-poms. Glue four white pom-poms to the body. Cut two black pom-poms in half. Glue the half pieces to the white pom-pom legs. Cut the ears, tail, and tongue out of felt and glue to the body. Glue googly eyes.

PATTERNS

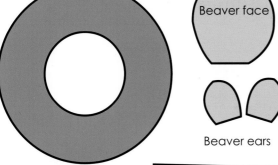

Beaver face

Beaver ears

Beaver feet

Beaver tail

Bird tail

Fold

Bird feet

Bird feather
cut 2 pieces

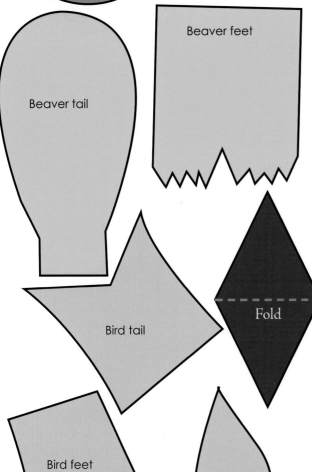

Pattern for the bean bag on page 22. (100 percent)

Fold

Fold

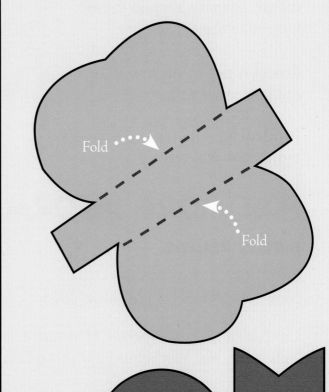

Pattern for the
carton critter on
page 18.
(100 percent)

Pattern for the
sock puppet on
page 9.
(100 percent)

Pattern for the
bumble bee on
page 30.
(100 percent)

Pattern for the
ostrich on
page 12.
(100 percent)

Pattern for the
bird on page 29.
Scaled to 50
percent.

Pattern for the
cardboard donut
on page 28. Scaled
to 50 percent.

Pattern for the
beaver on page 29.
Scaled to 50
percent.

Note: Three templates on page 31 are scaled to 50 percent of the original size.
Use a scanner or a printer to resize the templates. (200%)

31

GLOSSARY

dilute To make a liquid thinner by adding water.

dowel A peg or stick used to hold pieces together.

fundraiser An event held to make money for a charity.

retract To draw back in.

score To cut or scratch a line into a surface.

template A shape used as a pattern.

FOR MORE INFORMATION

FURTHER READING

Bull, Jane. *Crafty Creatures.*
New York, NY: DK Publishing, 2013.

Castleforte, Brian. *Papertoy Monsters: 50 Cool Papertoys You Can Make Yourself!*
New York, NY: Workman Publishing Company, 2010.

Chorba, April. *Pom-Pom Puppies: Make Your Own Adorable Dogs.*
Palo Alto, CA: Klutz, 2013.

WEBSITES

For web resources related to the subject of this book, go to:
www.windmillbooks.com/weblinks and select this book's title.

INDEX